Find Your Next Story on Every Page

Open Anywhere

CRIME WRITING PROMPTS

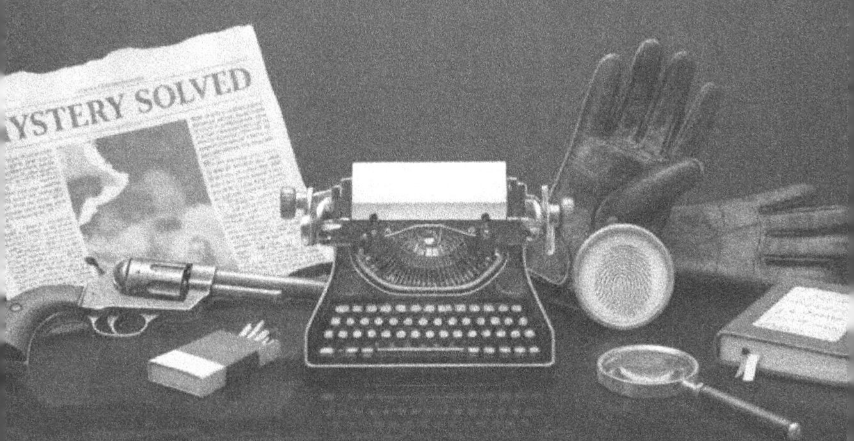

First published in Australia in 2025 by BookTree Publishing.

This pubwlication was created using a combination of human authorship and AI-assisted drafting. All content has been curated, edited, and shaped by the author.

ISBN: 978-1-7645951-3-1
Cover Designed: Adobe FireFly

Produced by Scribbly.com.au
Printed and bound in Australia by

BookTree
Publishing

PO Box 105
Narangba Qld 4504
Australia

www.booktreepublishing.com.au

A Note from the Author

Crime stories have always felt like locked rooms with hidden exits.

You can step into them quickly. You can leave them when the tension lifts. You can explore a single moment of suspicion without committing to a long investigation before you are ready. For many writers, crime is where confidence sharpens. It is where instinct begins to feel like intuition.

I created this collection after years of sitting beside writers — in libraries, workshops, quiet conversations, and online spaces — listening to the same question surface again and again: Where do I start?

The world is now full of crime prompts, tools, and technologies offering instant plot twists. That abundance can be exciting. It can also be overwhelming.

In developing this book, I made thoughtful use of modern tools — including AI-assisted drafting — to generate a wide field of possibilities. But this collection is not an automated list. It is a curated companion, built with care, tested with writers, and guided by lived experience in writing communities.

This book is not asking you to construct perfect crimes. It is offering you entry points into moments — clues, confrontations, quiet reveals — that you may follow at your own pace. Some will grip you immediately. Others will linger in the background. Trust that instinct. It is part of your voice taking shape.

If you write one complete crime story, that is powerful. If you write fragments, interrogations, or single scenes, that is equally valuable. Every sentence is a step deeper into the craft.

I hope these pages become a familiar place to return to. Remember: Crimes can be small and still compelling. Beginnings can be subtle. Writing can be deliberate.

Wherever your stories lead, I'm grateful you've invited this book into your investigation.

Warmly,

*For the writers of crime stories —
those who came before,
those writing now,
and those still gathering the courage to begin.*

Notes:

How to Use
This Collection

This collection was created for one simple reason: to help you write — not someday, not when life is quieter, but right now, with the time and energy you have.

Each book in this series follows the same pattern. Once you've used one volume, you'll know exactly how to use the next. No complicated rules. No theory-heavy lectures. Just open, choose a prompt, and begin.

Inside, you'll find clusters of prompts to spark ideas, creative boosters to shake things loose when you're stuck, and writing challenges to stretch you a little further when you're ready. Some days you might write for five minutes. Other days you'll disappear into a scene and look up hours later, surprised by what came out. Both count.

There's no correct order. No gold star for finishing every page. Some prompts will speak to you immediately. Others will wait patiently until you need them. Trust that.

Write messily. Write quickly. Write badly if you must. The magic isn't in getting it right the first time — it's in showing up at the page and letting the words find you.

So open anywhere.

Your next story is already waiting.

Quick Start Guide

There are no lengthy instructions waiting for you here, and no rules to follow. Only a gentle invitation to begin. Unsure how? Here is a suggestion to help you find your first step.

Step One — Open Anywhere: You can read in front-to-back order or let the book fall open where it wants to. Trust the page or prompt that finds you.

Step Two — Choose a Prompt: Read the cluster introduction. Skim the prompts. Notice which one gives you a tiny flicker of curiosity. That's your prompt.

Step Three — Set a Timer: Five minutes if you're busy. Twenty if you have the space. A full hour if you're disappearing into your story. Any time counts.

Step Four — Write Without Editing: Don't fix spelling. Don't reword sentences. Don't backspace. Let the words arrive however they arrive.

Step Five — Stop When the Timer Ends: Underline the sentence/s you like. Circle the idea/s you might return to. Close the book feeling proud that you showed up.

Other Ways to Use This Book

- Dip into the Creative Boosters when you're stuck

- Roll the Prompt Dice when you want surprise combinations

- Try the Writing Challenges when you feel ready to stretch Use prompts in writing groups or classrooms

- Return to favourite pages again and again

Always Remember:

Some days writing will feel easy. Other days it won't. Both are normal. The only real success is putting words on the page.

Open anywhere.

Start small.

Keep going.

Your stories are closer than you think.

A Note on Timers

Several of the challenges in this book suggest writing for a set period of time. For some writers, the word timer immediately conjures an image of a loud alarm, a ticking stopwatch, or pressure to race against the clock. That is not the intention here.

A timer is simply a boundary. A small agreement with yourself: for this length of time, I will stay with the page. Nothing more.

Your timer can be anything that marks passing time gently. A kitchen timer with the sound turned off. A clock on the wall. A playlist of three songs. The length of a cup of tea cooling beside you. Until the washing machine has finished.

Some writers prefer no device at all. They simply write until they feel a natural pause, then check the time afterward. This is equally valid.

The purpose of timed writing is not speed. It is permission. When the end point is known, the mind relaxes into the task. The inner critic quiets. Words arrive more freely.

Choose whatever method feels kind.

The page does not need urgency.

It only needs your presence.

Contents

Part One

WARM-UP & MINDSET

Notes:

Warm-Up & Mindset

Before beginning, it helps to pause for a moment and remember that writing does not require perfect conditions or elaborate preparation. It asks only for attention — a willingness to meet the blank space and see what might emerge.

This opening section is designed to settle you into that space. Nothing here is compulsory. You can skip this section if you wish. There are no rules to master before you proceed. This is simply a quiet threshold between intention and action.

Why Crime Writing Matters

Crime writing occupies a distinctive place in a writer's practice. It is structured enough to build tension, yet flexible enough to explore motive, consequence, and human behaviour. Within a few pages, you learn to identify what is at stake, to shape suspense, to follow clues, and to understand how revelations land.

For new writers, crime offers clear entry points — a mystery, a question, a disruption. For returning writers, it provides a way back to momentum. For experienced writers, it remains a testing ground — a place to experiment with pacing, perspective, and psychological depth without the long arc of a novel pressing overhead.

It is not uncommon for writers to discover their voice through a single crime scene written almost by instinct. Many larger works begin as fragments — an interrogation, a discovery, a moment of unease. Each piece you write strengthens your sense of structure and control, regardless of whether it is ever shared. Perfection is not the objective here. Awareness is.

Using This Collection

This book is intended as a working companion. It is not a course and not a curriculum. There is no prescribed order and no expectation that every prompt will be completed.

Each cluster contains a short introduction, a set of core prompts, optional expansions, and a challenge for those moments when you wish to push further.

Later sections provide creative boosters and structured exercises to draw upon when momentum slows or curiosity calls.

You may choose to move through clusters sequentially. Or you may open the book at random. Both approaches are equally valid. It can be useful to mark the pages that resonate so you can return to them.

The only requirement is that you follow what captures your attention.

Preparing Your Writing Space

Crime writing can happen anywhere. At a desk. At a kitchen table. In a notebook balanced on your knee. On a phone screen late at night. There is no single correct environment.

Choose a space that allows you to think without interruption. Gather whatever tools feel natural — pen, keyboard, timer, or none at all. The aim is not to create ritual, but permission.

When you sit down to write, you create a small divide in your day. On one side is everything else. On the other is the unfolding of a mystery.

That divide is where the work begins.

Five-Minute Warm-Up Prompts

When the mind feels crowded or uncertain, short warm-ups help unlock the first lines. Here is a quick exercise if you need it.

1. Describe a place where something feels wrong, but you can't explain why.

2. Begin with the sentence: I knew something wasn't right the moment I saw it…

3. List five details you might notice at a crime scene, then build a scene from one of them.

4. Write about an object that could be evidence.

5. Recall a moment when your instincts told you something was off.

At some point, every investigation begins.

Turn the page when you're ready.

Notes:

Part Two

The Core Prompt Collection

Notes:

The Core Prompt Collection

Crime stories rarely announce themselves. They begin with something small — a detail that doesn't fit, a moment that feels off, a question that refuses to be ignored. This section is the heart of the collection: a series of prompt clusters designed to bring those moments forward.

Each cluster explores a core element of crime writing — tension, disruption, secrecy, motive, and consequence. Within each, you'll find prompts to begin, expand, and deepen your ideas.

There is no expectation to complete everything. Follow what draws your attention. In crime writing, curiosity is often the first clue.

Open where you feel pulled.

Begin without hesitation.

Follow the thread.

Notes:

The Suspicious Beginning

Every crime story begins with a moment of disturbance — the instant when something no longer fits and the ordinary starts to fracture. It may be subtle or sudden, quiet or confronting. What matters is that a line is crossed, and the character moves forward without yet understanding the consequences.

The prompts in this cluster explore beginnings already in motion: questions without answers, tension already present, unease that has begun to take hold. Trust that shift. Let the opening draw you deeper before you try to solve what lies ahead.

Core Prompts

1. A character opens a door they were certain was locked.
2. The first sentence begins in the middle of an accusation.
3. Someone receives a message that was never meant for them.
4. A routine journey is interrupted by an unexpected passenger.
5. A character realises they are being watched — but cannot find the watcher.
6. A phone rings after midnight. No one speaks, but the line remains open.
7. A character finds an object they thought had been

destroyed.
8. A conversation begins with the words, "You need to hear this."
9. A character enters a room in their own home that feels unfamiliar.
10. A stranger uses the protagonist's name without introduction.
11. A character wakes with no memory of how they got there.
12. A gathering is interrupted by sudden, unsettling news.
13. A photograph surfaces that no one can explain.
14. A simple favour draws a character into something far more complex.
15. A letter arrives with no return address — and no clear sender.

Deep Dives

Some ideas invite a slower approach. Here are a few ways to extend a prompt — optional paths for when curiosity deepens, or when you feel compelled to follow the thread further.

Use them when the tension holds. Leave them when it doesn't. Both are part of the process.

1. Write the opening scene without explanation. Let meaning emerge through behaviour, dialogue, and detail.
2. Rewrite the same opening from another character's perspective. Notice what is revealed — and what is hidden.
3. Place the beginning in a distinctly Australian

setting — a quiet cul-de-sac, a stretch of country highway, a beach car park before sunrise, a train platform in winter — and allow the setting to influence the sense of unease.

The Weekly Challenge

Write a complete crime piece that begins with a disruption, however small. Let that single moment guide every decision that follows. When you finish, return to the opening and ensure it carries the tension that unfolds throughout.

Notes:

A Moment That Changes Everything

Not every turning point in a crime story arrives with sirens and urgency. Often, it emerges through something quieter — a detail that doesn't align, a hesitation in someone's voice, a choice made without full awareness, a silence that feels deliberate. Only later does the character recognise that this was the moment everything shifted.

The prompts in this cluster explore those subtle fractures. They invite you to write the scene where suspicion deepens — where one moment separates what seemed certain from what can no longer be trusted.

Resist the urge to solve too quickly. Stay inside the tension. Let the significance reveal itself.

Core Prompts

1. A character agrees to something they don't fully understand.
2. A truth slips out at the wrong time. Someone says, "You won't see me again."
3. A character witnesses something they were never meant to notice.
4. A door closes — and remains locked.
5. A familiar place suddenly feels wrong.

6. A character deletes a message before sending it — then realises it mattered.

7. Someone offers help that feels impossible to refuse.

8. A character begins to doubt their memory of a key event.

9. A casual remark raises unexpected suspicion.

10. A character chooses to stay when leaving would be safer.

11. A long-held assumption quietly unravels.

12. A character hears their name in a place they shouldn't be.

13. A promise is made under pressure — and cannot be undone.

14. A character understands a critical detail too late.

Deep Dives

Some moments benefit from closer attention. Here are a few ways to extend a prompt — optional paths for when the tension holds and you want to explore it further.

Use them when the scene feels alive. Leave them when it doesn't. Both are part of the process.

1. Write the turning-point moment in real time, slowing the scene to capture physical sensations, breath, sound, and subtle shifts

2. Remove all dialogue. Let the change unfold through action, environment, and internal

response.

3. Write the same moment twice: once as it happens, and once as it is remembered later — notice what is altered, omitted, or reinterpreted.

The Weekly Challenge

Write a crime piece where nothing overtly dramatic occurs — yet by the final paragraph, the reader senses that everything has changed. Let restraint carry the tension. Let implication do the work.

Notes:

Secrets and Evidence

Every crime story conceals something. A detail overlooked. A motive buried. A past deliberately obscured. Suspense is built not only on what is discovered, but on what remains hidden — and every revelation has the power to shift the entire investigation.

The prompts in this cluster explore concealment and exposure. They invite you to write within that tension — the space between suspicion and certainty — and the moment when that space gives way.

Allow the truth to surface in its own time — quietly, abruptly, or with consequence. Trust the character's response to shape the scene.

Core Prompts

A character discovers a letter never meant to be found.

Someone admits to a lie they have carried for years.

1. A character discovers evidence hidden in plain sight.

2. Someone confesses to a crime they were never suspected of.

3. A photograph reveals a clue that contradicts an alibi.

4. A child repeats something that links directly to a crime.

5. A character realises the case they believed solved is anything but.

6. A long-buried crime is exposed during a public moment.

7. A character overhears a conversation that implicates someone they trust.

8. A hidden weapon or piece of evidence is uncovered during an ordinary task.

9. A character is confronted with proof that changes the direction of an investigation.

10. A stranger reveals knowledge only someone involved could know.

11. A confession arrives after the damage is irreversible.

12. A character realises their memory of a key event is flawed — or altered.

13. Someone breaks under pressure and reveals what they know.

14. A revelation is delivered casually, but carries serious consequences.

15. A truth emerges that connects two seemingly unrelated crimes.

Deep Dives

Some moments benefit from deeper focus. Here are a few ways to extend a prompt — optional paths for when the tension holds and you want to explore further.

Use them when the scene feels alive. Leave them when it doesn't. Both are part of the craft.

1. Write the revelation scene twice — first showing the discovery of the evidence, then the immediate consequences for the character. Notice how the tension shifts.

2. Place the revelation in an everyday setting — a roadside stop, a suburban backyard, a quiet café — and let the contrast heighten the impact.

3. Write the moment of revelation without stating the truth directly. Let the reader infer it through reactions, behaviour, and small details.

The Weekly Challenge

Write a crime piece where a critical piece of evidence is never directly explained, yet by the final paragraph, the reader understands exactly what has been uncovered.

Notes:

The Stranger

In crime writing, a stranger is rarely just a passer-by. They carry uncertainty — an unknown history, a possible connection, a motive not yet revealed. Their arrival shifts the balance of a scene. They may be a witness, a suspect, or something far less clear. Whether they stay or disappear, they leave questions behind.

The prompts in this cluster explore encounters with the unfamiliar — chance meetings, unexpected arrivals, and the tension that comes from not knowing who someone really is or why they are there.

Let suspicion guide you. Allow the stranger to unfold gradually.

Core Prompts

1. **A stranger arrives asking questions about a crime no** one believes they know about.

2. A character sits beside an unfamiliar person who knows details they shouldn't.

3. Someone new joins a workplace just as an investigation begins.

4. A stranger recognises the protagonist — but under a different name.

5. A visitor stays longer than expected, avoiding certain topics.

6. A stranger offers help with a case — without

explaining why.

7. A new neighbour moves in and avoids all personal interaction.

8. A character meets someone who seems deeply familiar with a past incident.

9. A stranger leaves behind an item that could be evidence.

10. Someone unknown appears at a private gathering — and no one challenges their presence.

11. A character realises they've been followed by the same stranger more than once.

12. A stranger tells a story that closely mirrors an unsolved case.

13. Someone new enters a group and subtly shifts suspicion.

14. A character receives a warning from a stranger they cannot ignore.

15. A chance encounter repeats — too often to be coincidence.

Deep Dives

Some encounters invite closer attention. Here are a few ways to extend a prompt — optional paths for when the tension holds and you want to explore further. Use them when the scene feels active. Leave them when it doesn't. Both are part of the process.

1. Write the scene from the stranger's perspective instead of the protagonist's. What do they

notice — and what do they conceal?

2. Write the encounter using only dialogue. Let tone, pauses, and choice of words reveal intent.

3. Place the meeting in a distinctly Australian setting — a country pub, a suburban train platform, a coastal caravan park, a roadside servo — and allow the environment to shape the tension.

The Weekly Challenge

Write a crime piece where the stranger's true purpose is never fully revealed — yet their presence changes the direction of the story in a lasting way.

Notes:

The Ordinary Made Suspicious

In crime writing, the familiar is often where unease begins. A routine. A place. A habit repeated so often it fades into the background — until something shifts. A detail doesn't align. A pattern breaks. The ordinary starts to feel wrong, and that quiet disturbance is where tension takes hold.

The prompts in this cluster invite you to re-examine the everyday. To notice what has been overlooked. To stay with the moment long enough for suspicion to surface.

Let observation lead. Trust the smallest detail to open the door.

Core Prompts

1. A character notices a small detail in their home that suggests someone else has been there.

2. A routine commute feels different — and the character can't explain why.

3. A familiar meal contains something that shouldn't be there.

4. A common phrase is spoken in a way that feels like a warning.

5. A daily task uncovers something deliberately hidden.

6. A character observes a neighbour's routine and realises it has changed in a concerning way.

7. A familiar sound occurs at the wrong time.

8. A character finds an item in their pocket that could link them to something they don't remember.

9. An everyday object breaks — revealing something concealed inside.

10. A character catches their reflection and notices something out of place.

11. A routine phone call includes a detail that raises suspicion.

12. A familiar street feels altered — as if something has happened there.

13. A character overhears an ordinary conversation that hints at something serious.

14. A well-known scent triggers a memory tied to an unresolved event.

15. A character performs a daily action and realises it may have consequences they didn't anticipate.

Deep Dives

Some moments reward closer attention. Here are a few ways to extend a prompt — optional paths for when the tension holds and you want to explore further.

Use them when the scene feels active. Leave them when it doesn't. Both are part of the craft.

1. Write the scene focusing only on sensory detail

— sight, sound, texture, taste, smell — and allow suspicion to build naturally.

2. Write the moment twice: first as the character experiences it, then as an external observer might describe it. Notice the difference.

3. Set the scene in a recognisably Australian everyday environment — a suburban kitchen, a backyard clothesline, a corner shop, a beach walkway — and let the setting heighten the realism and unease.

The Weekly Challenge

Write a crime piece where nothing overtly dramatic occurs — yet by the final paragraph, the reader understands that something is no longer right, and cannot be undone.

Notes:

The Decision

In crime writing, every turning point is a decision — to act, to conceal, to speak, or to remain silent. Sometimes it is overt and immediate. Other times it is internal, barely visible — a line crossed in thought before it is crossed in action. Choice is where tension sharpens. It is where motive, fear, pressure, and consequence collide.

The prompts in this cluster explore those moments — impulsive, calculated, desperate, or inevitable — where a single decision alters the direction of a crime or an investigation.

Stay with the weight of it. Let the character feel what is at stake before they act.

Core Prompts

1. A character says yes to something they know is wrong.

2. Someone chooses to leave a scene without reporting what they've seen.

3. A character decides to reveal the truth — knowing it will have consequences.

4. A door stands open at a critical moment. They must decide whether to enter.

5. A character chooses to protect someone who may be guilty.

6. Someone decides to stay silent when speaking up could change everything.

7. A character destroys evidence that could solve a case.

8. A decision must be made before time runs out.

9. A character chooses to trust a person they suspect.

10. A carefully planned course of action is abandoned in a single moment.

11. A character chooses self-preservation over justice.

12. Someone decides not to intervene — and becomes part of what follows.

13. A character chooses to revisit a memory they have tried to suppress.

14. A decision is made without words — but with lasting impact.

15. A character takes the riskier path, knowing it may not end well.

Deep Dives

Some decisions deserve closer attention. Here are a few ways to extend a prompt — optional paths for when the tension holds and you want to explore further.

Use them when the moment feels alive. Leave them when it doesn't. Both are part of the process.

1. Write the decision entirely from within the character's thoughts. Let doubt, reasoning, and

hesitation unfold.

2. Write the same moment without internal monologue. Show the choice only through action and behaviour.

3. Place the decision in a distinctly Australian setting — a long country road, a coastal lookout, a suburban backyard at dusk, a quiet intersection — and let the environment reflect the tension.

The Weekly Challenge

Write a crime piece where the central decision occurs in the middle of the narrative. Use the remainder of the story to explore the consequences of that choice.

Notes:

The Disruption

In crime writing, disruption is where control breaks. A plan unravels. An assumption fails. A moment that should pass quietly instead shifts everything off course. It may be sudden or subtle, but its impact is immediate — forcing characters to react, conceal, or make choices they weren't prepared for.

Disruption is not always dramatic. It can be a missing detail, a delayed arrival, a piece of evidence that doesn't appear when it should. Whatever form it takes, it alters direction and raises stakes.

The prompts in this cluster explore those moments when something goes wrong — and cannot be easily corrected.

Let the disruption hold. Resist the urge to resolve it too quickly.

Core Prompts

1. A character arrives too late to prevent a crime.

2. A carefully planned operation is cancelled without explanation.

3. Someone unexpected appears at a critical moment in an investigation.

4. A power outage disrupts a scene where something important was about to be revealed.

5. A character loses a key piece of evidence.

6. A crucial conversation is interrupted before the truth is spoken.

7. Bad news arrives during what should have been a safe moment.

8. A character's transport fails, leaving them unable to reach a scene in time.

9. A message arrives that contradicts the entire case.

10. A character is prevented from carrying out a necessary action.

11. Someone breaks a rule that jeopardises an investigation.

12. A minor mistake escalates into a serious complication.

13. A character is forced into close proximity with someone they suspect.

14. An expected outcome becomes impossible.

15. A case begins one way — then shifts direction entirely.

Deep Dives

Some disruptions benefit from closer attention. Here are a few ways to extend a prompt — optional paths for when the tension holds and you want to explore further.

Use them when the scene feels active. Leave them when it doesn't. Both are part of the process.

1. Write the disruption as a chain reaction. Show how one misstep leads to another.

2. Write the disruption without revealing its cause immediately. Let characters respond before the full picture becomes clear.

3. Place the disruption in a familiar Australian setting — a school pick-up zone, a weekend market, a suburban gathering, a country train line — and let the normality heighten the sense of something going wrong.

The Weekly Challenge

Write a crime piece where the disruption arrives late in the narrative. Use the first half to establish control and expectation — then allow the interruption to reshape everything that follows.

Notes:

The Quiet Resolution

Not every crime story ends with arrests or clear answers. Some close with uncertainty — a case left open, a truth only partly understood, a consequence quietly accepted. A restrained ending allows the tension to linger. It trusts the reader to sit with what remains unresolved. It suggests rather than confirms. The prompts in this cluster explore conclusions that do not declare themselves — endings shaped by ambiguity, consequence, acceptance, or the quiet aftermath of what has already occurred.

Resist the urge to tie everything together. Let the final moment settle. Trust what is left unsaid.

Core Prompts

1. A character watches a suspect disappear into the distance.

2. A conversation ends before the truth is fully revealed.

3. Someone leaves a crime scene knowing they won't return.

4. A character realises the chance to act has passed.

5. A piece of evidence is put away — deliberately, and without explanation.

6. A character stands in a familiar place, now marked by what has happened there.

7. A promise to uncover the truth is remembered, but not fulfilled.

8. Someone falls asleep knowing the case will remain unresolved.

9. A character listens as a siren fades into silence.

10. A door closes softly at the end of an investigation.

11. A character accepts an outcome they cannot change.

12. A routine continues — but altered by what is now known.

13. A character reviews a file one last time, then sets it aside.

14. A final glance is exchanged between those who understand — or avoided entirely.

15. A story ends in the middle of an ordinary moment, with something unresolved beneath it.

Deep Dives

Some endings benefit from restraint. Here are a few ways to extend a prompt — optional paths for when you want to explore the quiet weight of a conclusion.

Use them when the moment feels complete. Leave them when it doesn't. Both are part of the craft.

1. Write an ending where the character does not speak. Let action, gesture, and observation carry the meaning.

2. Write the final scene without naming the

outcome or emotion directly. Allow the reader to interpret it.

3. Place the ending in a distinctly Australian setting — a beach at dusk, a veranda at night, a long country road, a suburban street under streetlights — and let the setting hold the final tone..

The Weekly Challenge

Write a crime piece that ends one sentence earlier than feels comfortable. Stop before the explanation. Let the silence carry the weight.

Notes:

Part Three

Creative Boosters

Notes:

Creative Boosters

Not every writing session begins with a blank page and a single prompt. Some days you already have a scene forming, a character whispering, or a fragment of dialogue waiting to be explored. On those days, what you need is not a beginning — but a spark that tilts what already exists into motion.

The tools in this section are designed to do exactly that. They are small narrative catalysts: twists, fragments, voices, objects, openings. You can use them on their own, combine several together, or layer them onto any prompt from the earlier clusters.

There is no correct method. Simply choose what draws your attention and allow it to alter the direction of your thinking.

A slight shift is often all a story needs.

1. Twist Generators

Every story benefits from surprise — not always dramatic, but meaningful. A twist reframes what the reader believes they understand. It creates depth, tension, or emotional contrast.

Introduce one twist into a scene or story:

1. A character has been lying about something minor — until it becomes significant.

2. Someone arrives earlier than expected.

3. A character realises they are not where they thought they were.

4. A promised event does not happen.

5. An apology arrives from the wrong person.

6. A character discovers they have misunderstood a relationship.

7. Something believed lost is found — or something believed found is lost.

8. A character overhears their own name in an unexpected context.

9. A planned confession is interrupted.

10. A character chooses not to reveal what they know.

11. Allow the twist to change direction, not simply add drama.

2. Character Sparks

Characters often arrive as fragments — a gesture, a habit, a contradiction. These sparks offer starting points for people who feel alive on the page.

Choose a character spark from the list below. Build a moment around it. Let the character reveal themselves through action rather than explanation.

1. A person who avoids mirrors.

2. Someone who keeps every receipt they've ever been given.

3. A character who speaks rarely, but always with precision.

4. Someone who is generous with strangers and harsh with family.

5. A character who is afraid of being forgotten.

6. Someone who laughs at inappropriate moments.

7. A person who carries an object for luck, without believing in luck.

8. Someone who cannot say no.

9. A character who collects endings — of books, relationships, conversations.

10. Someone who never asks questions.

Choose one. Let them move through a moment. Watch who they become.

3. Setting Sparks

Place is never neutral. It shapes mood, pace, and behaviour. These settings offer a foundation for scenes to unfold.

1. A nearly empty train platform at dawn.

2. A backyard during a summer storm.

3. A coastal town in the off-season.

4. A fluorescent-lit supermarket late at night.

5. A country road with no reception.

6. A school car park after the last bell.

7. A hospital waiting room.

8. A pub just before closing.

9. A living room where no one sits in the same chair anymore.

10. A beach at low tide.

Choose a place. Listen to its atmosphere. Allow the setting to lead the scene.

4. Object Prompts

Objects carry memory, weight, and emotional residue. Place one at the centre of a scene.

1. A key with no known lock.
2. A cracked phone screen.
3. A ring removed and placed on a table.
4. A handwritten note folded many times.
5. A suitcase that has not been unpacked.
6. A photograph with someone cut out.
7. A jacket left behind.
8. A cup with lipstick on the rim.
9. A children's toy found in an adult space.
10. A watch that has stopped.

Allow the object to influence action and thought.

5. Dialogue Starters

Sometimes a story begins not with description, but with a voice already speaking.

Begin a scene with one of these lines:

1. "I wasn't supposed to tell you."
2. "We need to talk — now."
3. "You don't remember, do you?"
4. "I thought you'd never come back."
5. "This isn't what you think it is."
6. "I'm leaving in the morning."
7. "Promise me you won't ask why."

8. "It wasn't meant to happen like this."

9. "You owe me the truth."

10. "Don't say anything. Just listen."

Let the conversation reveal what the narrator will not explain.

6. First-Line Hooks

The first sentence sets a tone, a question, or a direction. These openings are invitations rather than instructions.

1. The day began like any other, until it didn't.

2. I knew something was wrong before anyone spoke.

3. The message arrived at 2:17 a.m.

4. We agreed never to discuss that night again.

5. By the time I understood what I'd done, it was too late.

6. Nothing in that house stayed where it belonged.

7. I have never told anyone what really happened.

8. The stranger knew my name.

9. We were all pretending.

10. I didn't expect to be the one who stayed.

Select an opening. Step inside its promise. Follow where it leads.

Notes:

Part Four

Advanced Writing Challenges

Notes:

Advanced Writing Challenges

Wherever you've opened this book, you've encountered beginnings, moments, revelations, choices, disruptions, and endings. You have gathered sparks, fragments, characters, and places.

The challenges in this section are designed to gather those elements and apply gentle pressure — not to force creativity, but to strengthen trust in your instincts.

Each challenge introduces a constraint: time, perspective, limitation, or structural play. Constraints are not obstacles. They are focusing tools. They quiet the inner editor and invite momentum.

Approach these exercises with curiosity rather than performance. The goal is not to produce perfect stories.

The goal is to practice finishing.

1. The 30-Minute Story Sprint

A short story does not always need long preparation. Sometimes speed allows honesty to surface before self-doubt intervenes.

Preparation (5 minutes)

- Choose one setting from the Setting Sparks.
- Choose one object from the Object Prompts.

- Choose one dialogue starter.
- Write them at the top of your page.

Writing (20 minutes)

Set a timer. Write a complete scene in which:

- Two characters share a moment of tension or connection.
- The chosen object appears naturally in the scene.
- The dialogue starter is spoken at a turning point.
- The scene ends with a subtle shift in understanding.

Do not pause to edit. Let the story move forward without correction.

Reflection (5 minutes)

Underline one sentence that feels alive.

Circle one moment you want to explore further later.

Stop there. Completion is the practice.

2. Writing Under Constraint

Limitation sharpens attention. When certain tools are removed, others grow stronger.

Choose one constraint and write a short story within it:

- No dialogue.
- No internal thoughts.
- Only one setting.

- Only five sentences.
- No use of the words said, thought, or felt.
- Begin and end with the same image.
- Tell the story in reverse order.

Let your chosen constraint guide structure rather than restrict imagination.

3. Perspective Shifts

Every story holds more than one truth. Changing perspective reveals hidden dimensions.

Choose one of the following:

- Rewrite a previous story from another character's point of view.
- Tell the story from an observer who does not understand what is happening.
- Tell the story from someone remembering the event years later.
- Tell the story from the point of view of an object present in the scene.

Notice what emerges when the narrative lens moves.

4. Genre-Bending Stories

Short fiction is an ideal space for experimentation. A shift in genre alters tone, rhythm, and expectation.

Choose a story you have already begun — or start a new one — and write it as:

- A quiet domestic drama.

- A mystery with an unanswered question.
- A speculative or surreal tale.
- A comedic misunderstanding.
- A minimalist literary vignette.

Allow genre to shape the story's atmosphere without forcing cliché.

5. The Story-in-a-Day Challenge

This challenge is simple: begin and finish a story in one day.

Morning — Choose a prompt. Write freely for twenty minutes.

Afternoon — Continue the story. Bring it to an ending.

Evening — Read once. Make only essential corrections. Then stop.

Do not polish. Do not perfect. Let the story exist as is.

Completion builds confidence.

Confidence builds consistency.

Part Five

Bonus Writer Tools

Notes:

Bonus Writer Tools

Writing is not only about inspiration. It is also about returning — to the page, to the practice, to the unfinished fragment that suddenly feels alive again. The tools in this final section are designed to support that return.

They are simple by intention. They require no preparation, no explanation, and no perfect conditions. Use them when you feel stuck, when you feel playful, when you feel uncertain, or when you simply want to write without making too many decisions first.

Consider these pages your quiet back pocket — always available, always ready.

1. Prompt Dice Tables:

Chance is a generous collaborator. When you allow randomness to choose elements for you, expectation loosens and curiosity steps forward.

If you have a six-sided die, roll once for each table. If not, use a random number generator from one to six. Combine your results and begin writing.

Table One — The Encounter

1. A meeting at a train platform
2. A chance crossing in a supermarket aisle
3. A shared wait in a hospital reception
4. A conversation at a bus stop

5. An encounter on a quiet beach

6. A meeting in a café just before closing

Table Two — The Tone

1. Awkward politeness

2. Quiet curiosity

3. Unspoken tension

4. Unexpected warmth

5. Subtle irritation

6. Immediate familiarity

Table Three — The Complication

1. A misunderstanding arises

2. Someone leaves abruptly

3. A truth slips out

4. A third party interrupts

5. Time runs out

6. Something is forgotten

Table Four — The Object

1. A set of keys

2. A folded note

3. A mobile phone

4. A jacket

5. A photograph

6. A cup of untouched tea

Combine your rolls. Write a scene of 500 to 1,000 words. Allow the elements to guide the story rather than control it.

Example Roll

Table One: 2 — A chance crossing in a supermarket

Table Two: 4 — Unexpected warmth

Table Three: 3 — A truth slips out

Table Four: 6 — A cup of untouched tea

Resulting Prompt: Two people cross paths in a supermarket. Their interaction begins with unexpected warmth. During the exchange, a truth slips out. A cup of untouched tea is involved.

Begin writing.

2. Random Prompt Picker

On days when decision-making feels heavier than writing, let selection be effortless.

Close your eyes. Open the book at random. Place your finger on the page. Use the prompt beneath it. If no prompt sits there, use the nearest one above or below.

There is no wrong choice. The page you open is simply the one you needed today.

3. Monthly Writing Tracker

Consistency is built gently, not forcefully. A writing habit does not require daily output. It requires return.

At the beginning of each month, note the days you intend to write. Mark each day you do — even if only for five minutes. At the end of the month, look at what you accomplished rather than what you missed.

Momentum grows quietly. If you wish, the Monthly Writing Tracker on the next page provides a space to notice your rhythm over time.

Now you have reached the end of this section, this book closes — but your practice does not.

You now have beginnings, turning points, revelations, choices, disruptions, endings, sparks, challenges, and tools. All that remains is the return.

Open anywhere.

Begin again.

Open Anywhere

Monthly Writing Tracker

Monthly Writing Tracker

A writing practice grows through return, not force. This tracker is not a measure of productivity, but of presence. Mark each day you sit with the page — whether for five minutes or an hour. At the end of the month, notice what you did rather than what you missed. Small consistencies quietly build strong habits.

Month: ________________________

My intention for this month:

____

____

____

____

____

Writing Days (Tick each day you write, even little bits.)

☐ 1   ☐ 2   ☐ 3   ☐ 4   ☐ 5   ☐ 6   ☐ 7

☐ 8   ☐ 9   ☐ 10   ☐ 11   ☐ 12   ☐ 13   ☐ 14

☐ 15   ☐ 16   ☐ 17   ☐ 18   ☐ 19   ☐ 20   ☐ 21

☐ 22   ☐ 23   ☐ 24   ☐ 25   ☐ 26   ☐ 27   ☐ 28

☐ 29   ☐ 30   ☐ 31

What I worked on

One thing I discovered this month

A line I liked

Next month, I want to explore

Notes:

Notes:

Open Anywhere

Note Pages

Use the following pages to collect:

- Lines you like
- Character sketches
- Scene fragments
- Possible titles
- Observations from daily life

Return to these pages when a prompt calls for something new. Your own notes will become your richest resource.

MYSTERY SOLVED

MYSTERY SOLVED

MYSTERY SOLVED

MYSTERY SOLVED

About the *Open Anywhere* Series

Writing rarely begins with a perfect plan. More often, it begins with a spark — a half-formed idea, a sudden image, a sentence that arrives out of nowhere. The *Open Anywhere* series was created to honour that moment.

Each book in this collection is designed to meet you exactly where you are in your writing journey. No pressure. No prerequisites. No expectation that you call yourself a "real writer" before you begin. Just an invitation to open a page and let something new unfold.

Every volume follows the same trusted structure — prompt clusters, creative boosters, and writing challenges — so once you feel at home in one book, the others become familiar companions. The genres change. The sparks shift. But the rhythm stays the same: *choose, imagine, write.*

Some readers use these books for daily practice. Some dip in when they feel stuck. Some bring them to writing groups, classrooms, libraries, or quiet corners of cafés. However you use yours, know this: *the goal is not perfection. It's momentum.* It's experiencing the simple joy of putting words on a page.

The *Open Anywhere* series is part of a wider creative ecosystem built for writers — a belief that stories grow best in good company. Wherever you are on your writing path, you're welcome here.

So keep this book close. Return often. Let it surprise you.

And when you're ready for a new genre, a new challenge, or a new direction — there's another volume waiting.

Open anywhere. Your next story is already inside.

Where the Series Goes Next

The *Open Anywhere* series has been designed as a collection of companion books — each exploring different genres.

Future books are already taking shape behind the scenes. Others will emerge as writers like you reveal what they need next. When they arrive, they will be written in the same familiar format — ready to open at any page, ready to begin again.

Stay in Good Writing Company

These books are created through *Scribbly*, the writing community initiave from *BookTree Publishing*. If you'd like to hear when new books in the series are released — along with free resources, mentoring opportunities, and writing projects — you are warmly invited to visit us at www.scribbly.com.au

Our Invitation

Keep this book close. Return when the page feels quiet. Trust that every visit matters, and when the next volume appears, you will already know how to begin.

Open anywhere.

Your next story is already inside.

About the Author

Katy More is a writer, mentor, and creative guide with a deep commitment to helping writers find their way to the page — and stay there with confidence. She is the founder and creative heart of *Scribbly,com.au*, a quiet, supportive space for writers built on care, clarity, and community, and she brings practical experience from years of mentoring, editing, and writing across genres.

Katy also contributes her design and communications expertise to *BookTree Publishing*, where she helps authors navigate the journey from idea to finished book with calm purpose and clear guidance.

Across her work — in books, publications, blogs, workshops, and conversations — Katy has long championed the idea that storytelling need not be intimidating. She believes that short stories, in particular, offer writers a generous and immediate way into craft, voice, and creative momentum. Her approach blends thoughtful structure with room for discovery, encouraging writers to trust their instincts and return to the page without self-judgement.

Katy lives and works in Queensland, Australia, where she assists both emerging and experienced authors, leads community writing projects, and continues to develop resources that help writers feel seen, heard, and capable. She writes in her own name as well as through the diverse voices of the *Scribbly* collection, always bringing practical experience, curiosity, and support to every project.

About the Publisher

BookTree Publishing is an Australian independent publisher dedicated to helping writers bring meaningful books into the world — professionally, ethically, and with care.

Based in Queensland, *BookTree* works alongside authors at every stage of the publishing journey. Their focus is simple: practical pathways, transparent guidance, and publishing solutions that respect both the writer and the reader.

BookTree believes that publishing shouldn't feel mysterious or inaccessible. It should feel like a partnership — where ideas are nurtured, books are built well, and writers are supported to make informed choices about their creative futures.

Produced by *Scribbly*.com.au

Scribbly.com.au is the creative community and mentoring division of *BookTree Publishing* — a home for writers who want encouragement, resources, and good company along the way — all run by volunteers.

Through free mentoring, writing resources, workshops, podcasts, and community projects, *Scribbly* pairs experienced writing mentors with intelligent creative tools to support writers — from first tentative ideas to finished manuscripts and beyond. It is a place where curiosity is welcomed, questions are encouraged, and no writer is expected to walk alone.

The ***Open Anywhere*** series is an initiave of *Scribbly* — supported by *BookTree*— shaped by years of working directly with writers, listening to where they get stuck, what inspires them, and what helps them return to the page. These books are a natural extension of that mission: simple, friendly tools designed to help writers begin — again and again.

To learn more about *BookTree Publishing*,
visit: www.booktreepublishing.com.au

To explore *Scribbly*'s free writing resources,
visit: www.scribbly.com.au

Because stories grow best

in good company.